# MLA:
# The Easy Way!
## Eighth Edition

**Peggy M. Houghton, Ph.D.**
**Timothy J. Houghton, Ph.D.**

**Editors:  Sandra W. Valensky, Ph.D.**
**Michele M. Pratt**

*Education is one of the best investments you will ever make...*
*and our books maximize that investment!*
**Houghton & Houghton**

*Change the course.*

© Copyright 2016, 2008 Peggy M. Houghton, Ph.D.

Print edition 2016

Electronic edition 2016

ISBN: 978-1-93535-652-3

For more information, contact:

XanEdu Publishing

cust.serv@xanedu.com

800-562-2147

**Library of Congress Cataloging-in-Publication Data**

Houghton, Peggy M.

MLA : the easy way! / Peggy M. Houghton, Timothy J. Houghton; editor, Sandra W. Valensky, Michele M. Pratt.
    p. cm.
Includes index.
ISBN
1. Report writing--Handbooks, manuals, etc. 2. Research--Handbooks, manuals, etc. I. Houghton, Timothy J., 1961- II. Pratt, Michele M. III. Title.
    LB2369.H68 2008

808'.02--dc22

2008000949

**Manufactured in the United States of America**

# Table of Contents

# Preface

With more than 45 years of teaching experience, the authors of this handbook discovered students display considerable confusion with writing according to the Modern Language Association (MLA) guidelines. Those who are familiar with MLA format realize that many students are apprehensive and rather perplexed with this particular writing style.

Although MLA writing style is designed for those who intend to publish, numerous colleges and universities adhere to these stringent guidelines for student papers. Years of experience have proven to the authors that consistent questions and misunderstandings exist regarding this style. Consequently, this document has been developed to expand and enhance the MLA writing experience. Since some MLA guidelines are optional, the instructor should be consulted for final authority with regard to writing assignments.

*MLA: The Easy Way!* provides the most commonly required MLA rules in *one* easy-to-use guide, which does not require the user to search in multiple reference locations (i.e., book *and* website). This guide is divided into four parts: Mechanics of MLA, In-text Citations, The Works Cited Page, and a Sample Paper.

*NOTE:* Throughout this book, both single-spacing and boldface type have been utilized. Although this is not in accordance with MLA writing style, both have been used to simply save space and/or highlight specific rules. In addition, some names given throughout are fictitious.

# Part One

## Mechanics of MLA

### Setting Up a Document Using Microsoft Word
**(for Word 2007, 2010, 2013, and 2016)**

The following are specific instructions for setting up an MLA document using Microsoft Word 2007, 2010, 2013, and 2016.

### Margins

1. Select PAGE LAYOUT from the ribbon tabs. (*NOTE:* for Word 2016, the wording on the ribbon tab is LAYOUT.)

2. Click on MARGINS and Select NORMAL.

### Alignment/Line Spacing

1. Select HOME from the ribbon tabs.

2. Select the PARAGRAPH window (by clicking the icon to the right of the word *paragraph*).

3. Under ALIGNMENT, select LEFT.

4. Under LINE SPACING, select DOUBLE.

5. Under SPACING, set both BEFORE and AFTER to 0 pt. Click OK.

### Font Type and Size

1. Select HOME from the ribbon tabs.

2. Select the FONT window (by clicking the icon to the right of the word *font*).

3. Select an easily readable font such as Times New Roman.

4. Select SIZE 12. Click OK.

## Paragraph Indentation

1. Select HOME from the ribbon tabs.

2. Select the PARAGRAPH window (by clicking the icon to the right of the word *paragraph*).

3. At INDENTATION, set LEFT to .5". Click OK.

## Hanging Indentation

1. Select HOME from the ribbon tabs.

2. Select the PARAGRAPH window (by clicking the icon to the right of the word *paragraph*).

3. Under SPECIAL, choose HANGING. Under BY, select .5". Click OK.

## Page Numbering

Beginning on the first page and running continually throughout the MLA document, a running head should be utilized. This running head appears right justified, one-half inch down from the top margin, and includes the author's last name, one space, and the appropriate page number. This can be accomplished by using the HEADER AND FOOTER function:

1. Select INSERT from the ribbon tabs.

2. Select PAGE NUMBERS in the HEADER & FOOTER box.

3. Select TOP OF PAGE and the PLAIN NUMBER 3 example.

4. Type in the author's last name and one space.

5. Double click in the document and begin typing.

# First Page of MLA Document

At the left margin, one inch from the top of the page, the author's name, instructor's name, the course name and number, and the date are typed. Each element is double-spaced and typed on separate lines. Following these entries, the title is double-spaced and centered with all proper nouns being capitalized. The title should **NOT** be italicized, underlined, boldfaced, typed in all capital letters, or placed in quotation marks. Double-space between the title and the first line of the document.

First Page
of Document

Weibel 1

Ralph Weibel

Professor Hoban

English 320

23 April 2016

Principalship 101: Listening and Learning

from Faculty, Staff, Students, and Parents

# Setting up a Document Using Microsoft Word
## (for Word 2003)

The following are specific instructions for setting up an MLA document using Microsoft Word.

## Margins

All margins (top, bottom, and sides) are set at one inch. Microsoft Word allows the user to set the margin at a default of one inch. To do so, follow the guidelines below:

**Margins**

1. Under FILE, select PAGE SETUP.

2. Select MARGINS tab and type 1" at TOP, BOTTOM, LEFT, and RIGHT boxes. Click OK.

## Alignment/Line Spacing

All documents following MLA guidelines are required to be aligned left and double-spaced throughout the entire document. Do not include additional spacing. To set the default, follow these guidelines:

**Alignment/ Line Spacing**

1. Placing the cursor at the start of the document, select FORMAT.

2. Under FORMAT, select PARAGRAPH.

3. Under PARAGRAPH, set ALIGNMENT to LEFT.

4. Under PARAGRAPH, set LINE SPACING to DOUBLE. Click OK.

## Font Type and Size

The actual font type is an easily readable font such as 12-point Times New Roman.

**Font Type and Size**

To set both the font size and style using Word, do the following:

1. Under FORMAT, select FONT.

2. Under FONT, select Times New Roman.

3. Under SIZE, select 12. Click OK.

> This is an example of 12-point Times New Roman.

**Font Type and Size**

## Paragraph Indentation

Indent the first line of each new paragraph one-half inch. This can easily be accomplished by striking TAB on the keyboard. To set tab to a one-half inch default, do the following:

1. Under FORMAT, select PARAGRAPH.
2. Under PARAGRAPH, select TABS.
3. Under TABS, set DEFAULT TAB STOPS at .5". Click OK.

**Paragraph Indentation**

## Hanging Indentation

To set the hanging indentation feature for the *Works Cited* page, do the following:

1. Under FORMAT, select PARAGRAPH.
2. Under SPECIAL, choose HANGING. Click OK.

**Hanging Indentation**

> Simpson, John Henry, et al. *Changes in High School Theatrical Performances.* Grace, 2016.

## Page Numbering

Beginning on the first page and running continually throughout the MLA document, a running head is utilized. This running head appears right justified, one-half inch down from the top margin, and includes the author's last name, one space, and the appropriate page number. This can be accomplished by using the HEADER AND FOOTER function:

**Page Numbering**

1. Under VIEW, select HEADER AND FOOTER.
2. Select the page number icon (the first icon on the left with the # symbol); the number will appear on the left side of

the box. The cursor will appear to the right of the number. Move the cursor, using the left arrow key, to the left of the number. Press the spacebar once, thus moving the number correspondingly. Move the cursor to the left margin. At this point, type the author's last name.

3. Highlight the entire typed portion, including both the author's name and the number.

4. Hit the align right key located in the toolbar.

## First Page of MLA Document

At the left margin, one inch from the top of the page, the author's name, instructor's name, the course name and number, and the date are typed. Each element is double-spaced and typed on separate lines. Following these entries, the title is double-spaced and centered with all proper nouns being capitalized. The title should **NOT** be italicized, underlined, boldfaced, typed in all capital letters, or placed in quotation marks. Double-space between the title and the first line of the document.

Weibel 1

Ralph Weibel

Professor Hoban

English 320

23 April 2016

Principalship 101: Listening and Learning

from Faculty, Staff, Students, and Parents

# Part Two

## In-text Citations

The Modern Language Association (MLA) dates back to 1883. The goal of the *MLA Handbook* is to standardize practices for writers and researchers. This handbook is widely used among the humanities, but high schools and colleges have also accepted it as a formalized writing style for many other academic disciplines.

Guidelines for MLA in-text citations include the following:

### General Comments

- Use 8 ½ by 11 inch (non-erasable type) paper.

- All pages contain a continuous running head with the author's surname (upper and lowercase lettering) followed by one space and the page number (positioned one-half inch from the top and flush with the right margin).

- Margins are one inch around the entire document.

- Use left justification only (no right or full justification).

- Double spacing is used throughout the document. (Examples are single spaced in this book to save space.)

- Paragraph indentation is one-half inch (from the left margin).

- An easily readable type or font is used (example: Times New Roman -- 12 point).

- Bold type or font is not used.

- Print on only one side of the paper (not both sides).

- Automatic hyphenating features on word processing programs are turned off.

- *Anonymous* or *Anon* is not used (if no author is cited).

- Professional credentials, titles, affiliations, and degrees are not used (PhD, JD, MD, Sir, Lady, Saint, etc.).

- Suffixes that are essential parts of the name are included when referencing a person for the first time (Jr., Sr., III, etc.).

- The name of a news or wire service should not be used in place of the name of an author.

**General Comments**

- Works that are cited in text list the surname of the author(s) followed by the page number(s) where the work was found (in parentheses).

*NOTE:* Credit may be provided with either a signal phrase or a parenthetical citation.

> Valensky supported the motion (54).
>
> The motion was supported (Valensky 54).

- Titles cited in text are italicized and listed in upper and lowercase lettering.

- Appropriate credit must be provided or the work may be considered plagiarized (and result in serious academic consequences).

- All works cited in the text are cited in the *Works Cited* page. All works listed on the *Works Cited* page are cited within the text.

## Title Page

**Title Page**

- Do not use a formal title page.

- Cite the author's name, instructor's name, course name and number, and date in the upper left corner of the first page.

## Tables

- Use sparingly.
- Use as supplemental text material.
- Do not duplicate information already in the text.
- Assign arabic numerals and short titles.
- Locate as closely as possible to their mention in text.
- Include a short heading for every column.
- Use vertical spacing.
- Double space within.

Table 1

Animals Receiving Vaccinations in the United States

| Year | Beef | Pork | Chicken |
|---|---|---|---|
| 1998-99 | 11,314 | 10,416 | 876 |
| 1999-2000 | 12,134 | 10,745 | 912 |
| 2000-01 | 12,344 | 11,101 | 1,002 |
| 2003-04 | 13,332 | 12,118 | 1,136 |

Source: Dept. of Agriculture National Center for Agricultural Statistics: *Digest of Agriculture Statistics 2007*; United States Dept. of Agriculture. Mar. 2009, www.ncag.ed.gov/programs/read/d104/tables/dt08_443.asp.

## Numbers

- Numerals must be spelled out at the beginning of sentences.

> Nineteen eighty-four was a great year for the Detroit Tigers.

- Numerals are spelled out when only one or two words are utilized.

> four
>
> two thousand
>
> sixteen
>
> six million

- If the paper involves frequent use of numbers (scientific or statistical research), write as numerals.

> Alaska averaged 15 students per classroom, while Georgia and Texas averaged 8 and 12, respectively.

- Write numbers as numerals for more than two words.

> 7.45
>
> 607
>
> 93.57
>
> 49,670

- Commas are inserted between the third and fourth digits from the right, the sixth and seventh, and so forth.

- Exceptions include page and line numbers, four-digit year numbers, and addresses.

> 1,217
>
> on page 2017
>
> happened in 1999 and 2003
>
> 34,000
>
> 6,212,336
>
> located at 3112 East Tacoma

- Write numbers as numerals when preceding technical units of measure.

> 14 centimeters
>
> 9 grams
>
> 2000 gallons
>
> 21 amperes

- Write numbers as numerals for abbreviations, times, dates, addresses, pages, and symbols.

> 15 lbs.
>
> 135 12th Avenue
>
> page 13
>
> $11.34
>
> 5"
>
> 7:33 a.m.
>
> October 22, 1939
>
> 1313 Mockingbird Lane
>
> 4%

- Write numbers as numerals when comparing data.

> The meat packing cooler temperature ranged from 35 degrees to 43 degrees.

## Numbers (continued)

- Use numbers and words in combination for large numerals.

> 17.5 trillion dollars
>
> 2.45 million people

- Use lowercase roman numerals for book pages numbered such as the following:

**Numbers**

> page iii
>
> page xiv

- Use uppercase roman numerals for people's names.

> Henry VIII
>
> Milton Charles Houston IV

- Use the following for ranges of inclusive numbers. (Commas should not be used if the inclusive ranges are page numbers.)

> 1-6 *is used for* 1 through 6
>
> 21-26 *is used for* 21 through 26
>
> 32-55 *is used for* 32 through 55
>
> 97-101 *is used for* 97 through 101
>
> 119-21 *is used for* 119 through 121
>
> 925-1,007 *is used for* 925 through 1,007
>
> 1,009-31 *is used for* 1,009 through 1,031
>
> 1,788-896 *is used for* 1,788 through 1,896

## Page Numbers (as part of a parenthetical citation)

- Do not use *page*, *p.* or *pp.*
- Provide the full second number for page numbers through ninety-nine.

Page
Numbers

2-7 *is used for* page 2 through page 7

10-17 *is used for* page 10 through page 17

344-57 *is used for* page 344 through page 357

593-607 *is used for* page 593 through page 607

1743-55 *is used for* page 1743 through page 1755

## Quotation Marks

- Place quotation marks around words with special meaning or those purposefully misused.

Quotation
Marks

Kelly McDonald truly believed her "internal clock" was ticking.

Michael Thurgood's "friend" turned out to be different than originally anticipated.

- Use quotation marks for translation of foreign words. (Italicize the words being translated.)

In French, the term *garder au froid* means "keep refrigerated."

## Square Brackets

Square
Brackets

- Use square brackets around words that need to be in parentheses within parentheses.

The goal was to fill the stadium to capacity (for the second [night] game) so potential investors would be impressed.

## Italics

Italics

- Italicize titles.

*Management Innovations*

## Foreign Words in English Text

- Italicize foreign words in English text.

> He was more of an *enemigo* than a friend to the Spanish authorities.

- Exceptions to this rule include foreign words that are well known due to frequent use in the English language. (Consult a dictionary.)

**Foreign Words**

| | |
|---|---|
| ad hoc | e.g. |
| versus | amigo |
| et al. | laissez-faire |
| genre | siesta |

## People's Names

- State a person's name fully and accurately the first time it is used, and then use only his or her last name in subsequent references unless two people have the same last name. If two people have the same last name, list their names in full on subsequent references.

- Formal titles (Mr., Ms., Mrs., Dr., Professor, etc.) are not used when referring to people.

**People's Names**

*First Reference -- Subsequent Reference*
Michael James Martin, Jr. -- Martin
William Jefferson Hughes, III -- Hughes
Rachelle Harter-Magelli -- Harter-Magelli
Edgar Allen Poe -- Poe
Sigmund Freud -- Freud (not Dr. Freud)

# Titles of Works

- Italicize titles and use upper and lowercase lettering.

> *Post Modern Theory in Russia* (book)
>
> *The Influence of Productivity on Job Satisfaction: A Quantitative Retail Analysis* (paper)
>
> *Hamlet* (play)
>
> *A Collection of Poetic Melodies* (book of published poetry)
>
> *Obtaining a Boater's Safety Certificate in Iowa* (pamphlet)
>
> *Exile on Main Street* (compact disc)
>
> *Wall Street Journal* (newspaper)
>
> *US News and World Report* (magazine)
>
> *Green Acres* (TV program)
>
> *Nutcracker* (ballet)

- Use quotation marks for titles of works published within larger works.

> "The Fiction of Marcus Gallant" (essay)
>
> "The Generation after Generation X" (article)
>
> "The Changing of the Colors" (short poem)
>
> "The Children of Carriage Valley" (short story)
>
> "The United States Economy Prior to the Industrial Revolution" (book chapter)
>
> "Jeremy Goes to College" (TV episode)
>
> "War of the Worlds" (radio program)
>
> "Brown Sugar" (song)

## Titles of Works (continued)

- Do not italicize or use quotation marks for sacred writings.

- Italicize individual published editions of sacred writings.

> Bible
>
> King James Version
>
> Old Testament
>
> Upanishads
>
> *Gideon's Bible*
>
> Talmud
>
> Koran
>
> Luke
>
> *Talmud of the Land of Israel*
>
> *Upanishads: Selections for the Modern Reader*

- Do not italicize or use quotation marks for laws (or acts or political documents), musical compositions (identified by form, number, and key), series, societies, buildings, monuments, conferences (seminars or workshops), or courses.

> Bill of Rights
>
> Empire State Building
>
> NAMP Annual Convention
>
> University of Missouri Studies in Research Writing
>
> John Birch Society
>
> Communication 120
>
> Beethoven's Symphony no. 6 in A, op. 84
>
> Washington Monument

- Do not use italics, quotations marks, or capital letters for words indicating divisions of works.

preface

appendix

chapter 4

scene 8

introduction

index

act 2

**Titles of Works**

# Quotations

## Prose

- Use quotations marks and incorporate the quotation in the text if it is four lines or less. (Quotations can occur anywhere in the sentence.)

- If no parenthetical citation is needed, punctuation is placed inside the last quotation mark.

**Quotations:**
**Prose**

> Marisa Bernhard, in her pamphlet, *The World is an Oasis,* wrote the thought-provoking line, "We view the world not from the perception of others, but from the perception of self."
>
> During that period, Joanna Henderson experienced "the best days of her life" and "the worst days of her life."

- If a parenthetical citation is needed, the punctuation is placed after the citation, followed by the sentence punctuation.

> Marisa Bernhard, in her pamphlet, *The World is an Oasis*, wrote the thought-provoking line, "We view the world not from the perception of others, but from the perception of self" (12).
>
> During that period, Joanna Henderson experienced "the best days of her life" and "the worst days of her life" (32).

- Quotations longer than four lines require a colon or comma after the introductory phrase. Insert the blocked quotation (indented one inch from the left margin with no quotation marks).

- If a parenthetical citation is needed, a citation follows the punctuation at the end of the sentence.

- Doublespace the blocked text.

Trying to encourage everyone that the world actually is a wonderful place, Bernhard noted:

> The times may seem troubling, but they are
> actually an opportunity for improving life
> on this great planet. People of all nations
> can unite to overcome just about any type of
> obstacle they encounter. Differing cultures,
> societal norms, and customs actually
> strengthen us because they promote diversity.
> All people's ideas do not have to be the
> same. In fact, dissimilar thinking promotes
> the exchange of different viewpoints, which
> encourages the examination of differing
> perspectives for problem resolution. (21)

- If two or more paragraphs are quoted, the first line of each paragraph is indented an additional quarter inch.

- An exception is if the first sentence quoted does not begin a paragraph, then this paragraph is not indented.

Trying to encourage everyone that the world actually is a wonderful place, Bernhard noted:

> The times may seem troubling, but they are actually
> an opportunity for improving life on this great planet.
> People of all nations can unite to overcome just about
> any type of obstacle they encounter. Differing cultures,
> societal norms, and customs actually strengthen us
> because they promote diversity. All people's ideas do
> not have to be the same. In fact, dissimilar thinking
> promotes the exchange of different viewpoints, which
> encourages the examination of differing perspectives
> for problem resolution. . . .
>
> This is good information . . . so use it well and
> prosper. This world is an oasis, so use it to your
> advantage. . . .(21)

## Poetry

- Use quotation marks and incorporate in text if quotation is three lines or less. (Quotations can occur anywhere in the sentence.)

- Use a forward slash (with a space on each side) to separate individual lines.

- Parenthetical citations (with line numbers) are placed after the last quotation mark and before the punctuation at the end of the sentence.

> Painter's poem is framed with a sense of hopelessness: "We try in vain as time leaves us forever" (3).
>
> Johnson ponders, "What will happen to me this night / This is my concern in such complex circumstances" (12-13).

**Quotations: Poetry**

- Quotations longer than three lines begin on a new line (indented one inch from the left margin with no quotation marks).

- Parenthetical citations follow the punctuation at the end of the sentence.

> Martin's "Paradise Through Flight" is very detailed and descriptive:
>
> Elevation brings out the best in human beings.
> Spirit rises with altitude, as troubles erode.
> The euphoria experienced is overwhelming.
> Complete submersion in atmospheric pleasure.
> The soul is refreshed with a sense of newness and purity. (5-9)

## Drama

- Set off a quotation from the text for two or more characters in a play.

- Begin the dialog next to the character's name (all capital letters, indented one inch from the left margin). Follow the name with a period, and start the dialog.

- Indent all subsequent lines of a character's dialog an additional quarter inch.

- Start a new indented line when the dialog switches to another character (following the same guidelines for the first character).

- Follow prose and poetry guidelines for other aspects of formatting.

Stephen Mandrelli's screenplay for *The Fading Sun* suggests the harshness of the pioneer environment:

> TEX. I can't sleep on freezing ground.
> BILLY. That's not a bad thing because many
>     men who sleep here never wake up again.
> TEX. You mean they die from the cold?
> BILLY. The cold only makes things
>     uncomfortable. The Indians do the killing.
>     There's nothing worse than a Sioux brave
>     looking for revenge in the middle of the night.

# Punctuation (periods, question marks, exclamation points)

- Avoid exclamation points unless used in direct quotations.

- All punctuation is outside of the closing quotation mark unless it is part of the actual quotation.

**Quotations:**
**Punctuation**

> *Original* (taken from an article by Jeremy Sims)
> The health care situation in the United States is such that we need to take immediate action!
>
> *Quotation*
> Sims assaulted "the health care situation in the United States . . . " (12).
>
> Did Sims assault "the health care situation in the United States . . . " (12)?
>
> Intense drama followed Sims' assault on "the health care situation in the United States . . . " (12).
>
> Sims stated, "The health care situation in the United States is such that we need to take immediate action!" (12).

- Following are examples of periods and commas used with quotation marks:

> *Original*
> I can only say that on the surface my client appears to be guilty, but evidence will show otherwise.
>
> *Quotation*
> Roselli noted, " . . . on the surface my client appears to be guilty, but evidence will show otherwise" (142).
>
> *Original*
> If you take the time to read what I have written, you will better understand my position.
>
> *Quotation*
> " . . . take the time to read what I have written . . . ," he told me (63).

- If the quotation is a question, the question mark is placed inside the closing quotation mark.

> The president then asked, "Why is the data so inaccurate?"

- If the quotation ends a sentence that is a question, the question mark is placed outside the closing quotation mark.

> When does Robertson discuss "the power of the pen"?

- If the question mark occurs where a period or comma are typically utilized, the period or comma is omitted.

> "Have you ever felt the need to write instead of speak?" Robertson inquired.

- Use single quotation marks to set off a quotation within a quotation.

> Roselli noted, "On the surface the case appears to be an 'open and shut' one, but evidence will show otherwise."

**Quotations: Punctuation**

## Ellipses

- Sometimes writers omit words, phrases, or sentences from passages in order to convey information with shortened quotations.

- The resulting quotation must accurately represent the original source.

- An ellipsis within a sentence uses three periods (with a space before each and a space after the last).

- If a parenthetical citation is needed, it is placed after the last quotation mark, followed by the sentence punctuation (after the final parenthesis).

**Quotations: Ellipses**

## Ellipses (continued)

> *Original* (extracted from an article by Bernie Polen and Thomas Eckert)
>
>> Food safety, based on the seven principles of HACCP, protects the public from pathogens in our food supply, which is of great importance to many consumers.
>
> *With ellipsis*
>
>> Polen and Eckert indicate that "food safety . . . protects the public from pathogens in our food supply, which is of great importance to many consumers" (21).

- An ellipsis at the end of a sentence uses four periods (with no space before the first or after the last).

- An ellipsis at the end of a sentence with no parenthetical reference uses four periods (with no space before or after the last). An ellipsis with a parenthetical reference uses three periods (with no space before or after the last).

> *Original* (extracted from an article by Bernie Polen and Thomas Eckert)
>
>> Food safety, based on the seven principles of HACCP, protects the public from pathogens in our food supply, which is of great importance to many consumers.
>
> *With ellipsis*
>
>> Polen and Eckert indicate that "food safety, based on the seven principles of HACCP, protects the public from pathogens in our food supply . . . " (21).

## Author-Page Citations

- Following are examples of books, magazine articles, or journal articles with single authors (cited in text or in a parenthetical reference).

> Wyman noted that The Rolling Stones are truly one of the greatest rock bands ever (152).
>
> The Rolling Stones are truly one of the greatest rock bands ever (Wyman 152).

- Following are examples of books, magazine articles, or journal articles with multiple authors (cited in text or in a parenthetical reference).

- Use *et al.* if the work has more than two authors.

- Spell out the word *and*.

> Scholars such as McLean, Tempest, and Williams support opposing viewpoints (135-46).
>
> Other scholars support opposing viewpoints (McLean, Tempest, and Williams 135-46).
>
> Women were found to be more productive than men in jobs involving human contact (Sears et al. 241-43).

- Following are examples of quotations from a book, magazine article, or journal article (cited in text or in parenthetical reference).

> Monte concluded productive workers were "satisfied" and "motivated" (126), while Turgot found them to be "committed" (112).
>
> As Simpson states, "Diversity is needed in order to achieve personal and professional goals . . . " (216).
>
> It is likely true "diversity is needed in order to achieve personal and professional goals . . . " (Simpson 216).

## Author-Page Citations (continued)

- When citing an entire work without page numbers (print, non-print, performance, or electronic publication), the title is italicized in text (rather than cited in a parenthetical reference) or simply referred to using significant individuals (authors, editors, directors, performers, etc.).

> *In text*
>
> Cyman's *Watchful Eyes of Society* offers compelling detail about the security of the United States.

- For multiple works by the same author (cited in text or in parenthetical reference), cite the author, title (italicized), and page numbers.

**Author-Page Citations**

> Many people experience trauma based on childhood experiences (Jones, *Psychology Today* 121-34).
>
> In *Psychology Today*, Jones indicates that many people experience trauma based on childhood experiences (121-34).
>
> Jones notes that many people experience trauma based on childhood experiences (*Psychology Today* 121-34).

- For authors with the same last name, use the first initial and last name (or full name) in all references.

> Edward Johnson believes the surge in China's economic growth will be short lived (17).
>
> Other economists believe China is destined to reach much higher levels of prosperity (T. Johnson 48).

- For an unknown author, cite the full title in text or a shortened version of the title in a parenthetical reference. (Use quotation marks for article titles and italics for book, newspaper, periodical, etc. titles.)

> *In text*
>
> According to the article, "The Times are Changing, Now More than Ever," people need to make sacrifices in their careers if they hope to advance (22).
>
> People need to make sacrifices in their careers if they hope to advance ("The Times are Changing" 22).

- For whole volume work cited in a parenthetical reference, cite the author (with a comma), and *vol.* (before the number).

- For whole volume work cited in text, write the word *volume* (before the number).

> The legal system provides justice for victims of this type of crime (Smith, vol. 3).
>
> In volume 3, Smith claims the legal system provides justice for victims of this type of crime.

- For a corporate author or government publication, cite the author and page number(s).

> The United States Department of Justice reported the Commercial Retail Workers Union (CRWU) is completely against merit based wage increases (22).
>
> A recent report stated the Commercial Retail Workers Union (CRWU) is completely against merit based wage increases (United States, Dept. of Justice 22).

- Electronic and online sources typically do not have page numbers, so cite the author.

- Cite *par.* (before the paragraph number) in a parenthetical reference if the source uses a paragraph numbering system.

> *Electronic source without numbered pages:*
> Response to the drug varied dramatically (Robbins).
>
> *Electronic source with numbered paragraphs:*
> Substance abuse is not limited to urban areas (Confetti, par. 4).

## Author-Page Citations (continued)

- For novels or plays, add helpful information such as chapter numbers (in addition to page numbers).

- Cite page number first (with a semicolon), then *ch.* (before the chapter number).

- List the chapter number or a similar designation if that is the only information available. List page numbers if available.

**Author-Page Citations**

> Nicholas Rachlinski appears in *The Money Game* as a man obsessed with wealth, yet afraid to take any of the risks necessary to achieve it (185; ch. 1).
>
> In *The Heart Beats Slowly*, Sara Bordeen grudgingly accepts her fate in an arranged marriage (ch. 2).

- For sacred writings (Bible, Torah, Koran, Sermons, etc.), cite the book, and separate the chapter and verse with a period.

> In the Bible, Jesus states, "For God so loved the world that he gave his one and only Son, that whoever believes in him shall not perish but have eternal life" (John 3.16).

- For a personal interview, cite the person's name (in text or in a parenthetical reference).

> Guitarist Jeff Beck discussed changes in his lifestyle over the past four decades.
>
> "My lifestyle had to change, or I would not be here today" (Beck).

# Avoiding Plagiarism

Plagiarism is a growing problem in educational institutions both domestically and internationally. The word *plagiarize* is defined in *Merriam Webster's Collegiate Dictionary* (10th edition) as, "to steal and pass off (the ideas or words of another) as one's own" (888).

Plagiarism can take one of two forms: intentional or unintentional. When a writer knowingly uses other authors' works without providing appropriate reference citations, he or she is intentionally plagiarizing. If, on the other hand, a writer uses others' thoughts or ideas and does not realize that credit must be provided, he or she is guilty of unintentional plagiarism. Unfortunately, both types of mistakes can result in serious academic consequences. When plagiarism occurs, some institutions may require that the student receive a failing assignment grade; others may insist on a failing course grade; others may place the student on academic probation; and, in extreme cases, some institutions may actually expel the student.

It is incumbent on the writer to be forthright and honest with regard to using original and/or existing writing. Plagiarism can be easily avoided if the writer simply provides appropriate credit when borrowing ideas or citing directly from another individual's work.

When paraphrasing (rewording) work from another author, the writer must provide credit to the person who developed the original work. This simply acknowledges the fact that the paraphrased material was the work of another individual. It is not primary data (original); rather it is secondary data (information already in existence).

**Avoiding Plagiarism**

Likewise, when citing a direct quotation, appropriate credit must be given. Again, this signifies that the quotation is provided by another individual. When citing verbatim (using another person's exact wording), the borrowed material must be placed in quotation marks and properly cited.

# Part Three

## The Works Cited Page

E very MLA document should include a works cited section at the end of the document listing all references. Every reference cited in the text should be listed on the Works Cited page, and every reference listed on the Works Cited page should be cited in the text.

References allow readers to find and utilize sources cited in text. References also indicate the vigilance of the writer, so particular attention should be paid to details (spelling, punctuation, publication dates, accuracy, etc.). Most importantly, references give proper credit to authors for their work.

Guidelines for the MLA Works Cited page include the following:

### General Comments

- Use 8½ by 11 inch (non-erasable type) paper.

- The heading is *Works Cited* (centered, in upper and lowercase letters).

- All pages contain a continuous running head with the author's last name followed by one space and the page number (positioned one-half inch from the top and flush with the right margin).

- Margins are one inch around the entire document.

- Use left justification only (no right or full justification).

- Entries are double spaced between and within. (Examples are single spaced in this book to save space.)

- An easily readable type or font is used (example: Times New Roman -- 12 point).

- Bold type or font should not be used.

- Print only on one side of the paper (not both sides).

**General Comments**

- The first line is flush left, with the following lines (if any) indented one-half inch (hanging indentation).

- Automatic hyphenating features on word processing programs are turned off.

- Entries are listed in alphabetical order by authors (using surname of first author, followed by surname of second author, etc.), associations (if the work is authored by an organization), or titles (if the author is unknown or the work is anonymous).

- *Anonymous* or *Anon.* is not used if no author is cited.

- Professional credentials, titles, affiliations, and degrees are not used (PhD, JD, MD, Sir, Lady, Saint, etc.).

- Suffixes that are essential parts of the name (Jr., Sr., III) are included after the given name, preceded by a comma (Hartness, Andrew T., Jr. or Saad, Michael James, III).

- Titles are italicized and in upper and lowercase lettering.

- If no publication date is given, then speculate the date with square brackets around it. Insert circa before the date if it is approximate, and insert a question mark (?) after the date if it is uncertain.

| | |
|---|---|
| [*circa* 2014] | is used for an estimated date of 2014 |
| [2014?] | is used for an uncertain date of 2014 |

## Numbers

**Numbers**

- Titles beginning with a numeral are spelled out.

| |
|---|
| "Three Cheers for Joe Stiver's Market Beating Strategies" |

## Page Numbers

- For numbers within a range, write the second number in full through ninety-nine.

- Page numbers are listed as follows:

1-9 *is used for* page 1 through page 9

12-19 *is used for* page 12 through page 19

33-42 *is used for* page 33 through page 42

249-56 *is used for* page 249 through page 256

492-503 *is used for* page 492 through page 503

Page
Numbers

- Do not underline or italicize.

## Abbreviations

- Acceptable abbreviations for months are the following:

Jan. *is used for* January

Feb. *is used for* February

Mar. *is used for* March

Apr. *is used for* April

May *is used for* May

June *is used for* June

July *is used for* July

Aug. *is used for* August

Sept. *is used for* September

Oct. *is used for* October

Nov. *is used for* November

Dec. *is used for* December

Abbreviations:
Months

**Publishers**

- In general, give only enough information for the reader to look up the publisher. For example, use Houghton for Houghton Mifflin Co. However, if (1) writing a bibliographic study or (2) history is important to the paper, list the publisher's name in full.

- Omit *A, An,* and *The* when used as an introductory word in a publisher's name.

> Daniels *is used for* The Daniels Co.
>
> Atlas *is used for* An Atlas Company
>
> Runkel *is used for* A Runkel Firm

- Omit *Corp., Co., Inc., Ltd.,* and *LLC.*

> Johnson *is used for* Johnson Corp.
>
> Bethanials *is used for* Bethanials, LLC.
>
> Dewitt *is used for* The Dewitt Co., Ltd.

- Omit *Press* (use *P*).

> Baltimore UP *is used for* Baltimore University Press

- Use familiar letter abbreviations instead of full publisher names.

> MLA *is used for* The Modern Language Association of America
>
> UMI *is used for* University Microfilms International
>
> ERIC *is used for* Educational Resources Information Center

- Other abbreviations:

> ed. *is used for* edition
>
> 2nd ed. *is used for* second edition
>
> vol. *is used for* volume
>
> supp. *is used for* supplement

| | |
|---|---|
| P *is used for* Press<br>U *is used for* University<br>UP *is used for* University Press<br>p. *is used for* page<br>pp. *is used for* pages<br>trans. *is used for* translation<br>par. *is used for* paragraph<br>no. *is used for* number<br>rev. *is used for* revised<br>sec. *is used for* section | **Abbreviations:<br>Other** |

## When Listing by Author(s)

- First, last, and middle names are used (if available).

| | |
|---|---|
| An article authored by Michael Eugene Comos:<br>    Comos, Michael Eugene.<br>An article authored by Michael E. Comos:<br>    Comos, Michael E.<br>An article authored by Michael Comos:<br>    Comos, Michael.<br>An article authored by M. E. Comos:<br>    Comos, M. E. | **Listing by<br>Author** |

- For one author note the following example:

Hartness, Andrew. *Socializing on College Campuses.* U of Michigan P, 2015.

- Sources with multiple authors use et al.

Sienkiewicz, John Henry, et al. *Great High School Athletes Transition into Coaching Roles.* Harper, 2015.

*Note:* Invert the first author's name but not subsequent authors.

## When Listing by Author(s)

- For multiple citations by the same author(s) use the following:
    - List the name(s) in the first entry only.
    - Type three hyphens in each additional entry (to represent the name or names) followed by a period.
    - List entries in alphabetical order by title.

> Peters, Barbara J., and Michael Bojelay. *Commercial Real Estate Bargains*. Johnson Publishing, 2013.
>
> ---. *Light Industrial Real Estate Bargains*. Johnson Publishing, 2015.
>
> ---. *Residential Real Estate Bargains*. Johnson Publishing, 2004.

**Listing by Author**

- For multiple citations by the same first author, list in alphabetical order by the second author's surname.

> Talbot, Brian Patrick. *Marketing Retail Cosmetics in California*. Buffalo State UP, 2015.
>
> Talbot, Brian Patrick, and Mitchell Clawson. *Bridging the Engineering and Packaging Gap in Cosmetic Manufacturing*. Buffalo State UP, 2004.
>
> Talbot, Brian Patrick, and Jeffery Peace. *Retail Trends in California*. Buffalo State UP, 2013.

- For corporate, unknown, or anonymous author(s), list by the title or association.

> *Eastern States Public Library Association Desk Reference*. Signet, 2015.
>
> *Encyclopedia of the Midwestern States*. McGraw, 2014.
>
> National Research Team for Drug Abuse. *Cocaine Reality in Rural America*. McGraw, 2015.
>
> *Nicky Hopkin's Solo Piano Projects*. U of California P, 2015.

## Books

- Detailed entries are generally listed in the following order (some or all of these might be applicable):

  Author(s)

  Title (italicized)

  Editor(s), translator(s), or compiler(s)

  Edition

  Volume(s)

  Series

  Publisher

  Publication date

  Location (pages, URL, etc.)

- In general, list author(s), title (italicized), publisher, and publication year information.

**Book Entry**

> Hoban, Donna M. *Medical Methodology for Combating Migraine Headaches*. Houghton Books, 2015.

- See the section *When Listing by Author(s)* for one author, multiple authors, multiple citations by the same author(s), multiple citations by the same first author, unknown or anonymous author(s), and unknown or anonymous author(s) with no publisher.

- For an edited compilation or anthology, note the following example:

> Frank, Donald, editor. *From Past to Present: Forty Years of Sound Distribution Advice*. Random House, 2015.

**Book Entry: Anthology**

- For a compilation or anthology (play, short story, poem, essay) note the following example:

> Poe, Edgar Allen. "The Raven." *The World's Finest Poetry*. Edited by Brice Drogasch. U of Cincinnati P, 2013.

## Books (continued)

**Book Entry: Translation**

- For a translation note the following example:

> Terry, Lisa Ellen. *The Sander's Codes*. Translated by Don Lewandowski. Kreissl Books, 2013.

- For an edited edition, note the following example (1974 is the original publication date and 2014 is the edited edition date):

> Danielson, Lillian Mae, editor. *The Real Story Behind Viet Nam*. By James Treblune. 1974. U of Iowa P, 2014.

**Book Entry: Edition**

- For an edition, note the following example:

> Tranchida, Peter J. *Practicing Law in Michigan*. 2nd ed. Wayne State UP, 2015.

- For one volume, note the following example:

> Prohaska, Paul. *Formulas of a Master Sausage Maker*. Edited by Thomas P. Eckert. Vol. 7. Cambridge UP, 2015.

**Book Entry: Volume**

- For two or more volumes, note the following example:

> Mitchell, Riley. *The American Encyclopedia of Professional Hockey*. Edited by Brett T. Houghton. 3 vols. Michigan State UP, 2014.

**Book Entry: Series**

- For a series, note the following example (12 is the series number):

> Hemler, Erin M., editor. *Learning the Art of Ballet*. Art of Dance. Vol. 12. U of Michigan P, 2015.

- For page numbers, note the following example:

> Jagger, Michael P. Afterword. *The Life of a British Rock Star*. By John Sapienza. Harmony, 2014. pp. 243-51.

**Book Entry: Article**

- For a signed article in a familiar reference book, note the following example:

> Lapensee, Dennis L. "Planet Earth." *Encyclopedia Britannica.*
> 27th ed. 2015.

- For an unsigned article in a familiar reference book, note the following example:

> "Plantation Soil." *Encyclopedia Americana.* 2014 ed.

## Brochures and Pamphlets

- In general, list like a book.

> Boston Symphony. *The Music of Jason Stein.* Barnes, 2015.
> *Food Safety at Home.* NSF, 2015.
>
> Audobon Society. *Wild Birds of North Carolina.* Johnsonville,
> 2013.

## Government Publications

- In general, if the author, editor, or compiler is known, list first. If the agency bears more importance, the author, editor, or compiler is placed after the title.

- If the author, editor, or compiler is unknown, list the issuing government agency first.

- Conclude with the title (italicized), publisher, and publishing year.

> England. Ministry of Agriculture. *Food Security Threats Within.*
> MPO, 2014.
>
> Pennefather, Michael Martin, compiler. *Catalog of FDA Staphy-
> lococcus Publications, May 4, 1991-July 20, 2013.* GPO, 2015.
>
> United States. Dept. of Education. *Education Variances in Public
> Schools.* GPO, 2014.
>
> United Nations. *Manufacturing Progress in Developing Nations.*
> McGraw Books, 2015.

## Published Proceedings of a Conference

- In general, list like a book with added significant information.

**Conference Proceedings**

Somerset, Daniel S., and Anthony Randazzo, editors. *Proceedings of the Forty-Ninth Annual Meeting of the Supernatural Phenomenon Society, June 11-16, 2013: Open Discussion Session.* Parker, 2015.

## Published Dissertations

- In general, list like a book with significant information added before the publication facts.

- Use *UMI* if published by University Microfilms International.

**Dissertations**

Parnello, James A. *The Influence of Post Traumatic Stress on African American Korean War Veterans.* Dissertation. U of Florida, 2013. UMI, 2003.

## Unpublished Dissertations

- In general, enclose title in quotation marks without italicizing.

Sauls, Patrick K. "A Comparative Study of CEO Ethics in Non-Profit Organizations." Dissertation. U of Missouri, 2013.

## Journals (with continuous pagination throughout annual volumes)

- Do not punctuate after listing the journal title.

- In general, list the author(s), article title (in quotation marks), journal title (italicized), volume number, issue number, publication date, and page numbers.

- See the section *When Listing by Author(s)* for one author, multiple authors, multiple citations by the same author(s), multiple citations by the same first author, unknown or anonymous author(s), and unknown or anonymous author(s) with no publisher.

> Andrews, Christine A. "What is the True Meaning of Spousal Psychological Warfarc?" *Marriage and Counseling Review,* vol. 12, 2014, pp. 389-401.
>
> Hendrix, James Marshall. "An Analysis of Change in Pop Music Culture." *Journal of Contemporary Music,* vol. 21, 2015, pp. 253-67.

**Journals**

## Journals (without continuous pagination)

- Some journals do not number pages continuously.

- In general, follow the guidelines for journals with continuous pages, but list first page number and a plus sign (+).

> Marcelli, Linda M. "Gender Stereotypes in Manufacturing." *Journal of Management,* vol. 14, no.3, 9 Oct. 2014, pp 14+.
>
> Mickelberry, Claude Charles. "A Comparative Analysis of Leadership Styles." *Leadership Quarterly,* vol. 13, no. 2, June 2013, pp. 12+.

## Journals (using only issue numbers)

- Some journals do not use volume numbers, choosing instead to use issue numbers only.

**Journals**

- In general, follow the guidelines for journals (with continuous pagination), but treat issue numbers the same as volume numbers.

LeFrank, Kathleen L., et al. "The Influence of High School Relationships on Adulthood Friendships." *Journal of Social Commentary,* vol. 21, 2013, pp. 119-32.

## Reviews (of books, performances, or films)

- In general, list the reviewer (if applicable), title of review (in quotation marks, if applicable), title of the work reviewed (italicized), author (editor, translator, director, etc.) of the work reviewed, publication title (italicized), publishing date (day, month, and year), and pages.

**Reviews**

Mingles, Zachary L. "American Classics." Review of *Brave Hearts of Early American Pioneers,* by Anthony Zuccaro. *New Republic,* vol. 12, Aug. 2014, pp. 23-34.

Mellworth, Randy. "New Movie Roles for Television Actors." Review of *Bright Lights in Big Cities*, director Benjamin Wells. *Tallahassee Herald,* vol. 17, Jan. 2013, late ed., p. D1.

Review of *Anthology of Modern Dance*, editors James Sellman and Gwen M. Barrett. *Times Literary Supplement,* vol. 5, Sept. 2014, pp. 231-43.

# Newspapers

- In general, list the author (if signed), article title (in quotation marks), newspaper (italicized), publication date (complete day, month, and year), edition, and page numbers.

- Do not list volume or issue numbers.

- List the city in square brackets (not italicized) if not included in newspaper name.

**Newspapers**

- Add the edition (if listed) after the date.

- Do not list a wire or news service as the author; do not list *Anonymous*.

- If the article is not printed on consecutive pages, list the first page number and plus (+).

"Delphi Plant Closing Affects Thousands." *Daily News* [Detroit], 13 Nov. 2015, late ed., pp. A2-3.

Skrock, Linda. "The Pennant Race Heats up in Boston." *Boston Herald,* 28 Aug. 2015, early ed., pp. C1+.

# Editorials

- In general, list the author (if signed), title (in quotation marks), source (italicized -- newspaper, magazine, etc.), publication date (complete day, month, and year), edition (if applicable), and page numbers.

**Editorials**

- List *Editorial.* after the title (before source).

Hardy, George. "American Teenagers and Morals." Editorial. *Newsweek,* 12 Jan. 2013, pp. 21-24.

"Underage Drinking on College Campuses." Editorial. *Denver News,* 14 April. 2015, early ed., p. C4.

## Magazines

**Magazines**

- In general, list the author (if signed), article title (in quotation marks), magazine title (italicized), publication date (complete day, month, and year if available), and page numbers.
- Do not list volume or issue numbers.
- If the article is not printed on consecutive pages, list the first page number and plus (+).

> "Careers in Veterinary Science." *Animal Welfare,* June-July 2015, pp. 16-18.
>
> Morelli, Stephanie. "New Retirement Strategies for Baby Boomers." *Money Management,* May 2014, pp. 115-21.
>
> Presnal, Peter K., and William Gates. "Website Design for Small Business." *Savvy Tech,* 6 March 2015, p. 22+.

## Television Series or Radio Programs

**Television or Radio Programs**

- In general, list episode or segment title (in quotation marks), significant individuals (performers, directors, narrators, producers, etc.), program title (italicized), series title (if any), network, call letters, and broadcast date (day, month, and year).

> "Ice Skating on Michigan Shorelines." Narr. Annie Hughes. Prod. Harmen Miller. Dir. Nicholas Bently. *Winter Sports Documentaries.* NBC. WDRQ, 17 Jan. 2015.

## Music Videos

**Music Videos**

- In general, list performer, song title (in quotation marks), album title (italicized), manufacturer, date of song, significant individuals (director, producer, etc.), and channel.

> Richards, Keith. "Eileen." *Main Offender.* Virgin, 1988, VH1.

## Sound Recordings

- In general, list the emphasized individual (artist, composer, conductor), title of recording (italicized), performers (if applicable), date of recording (if available), manufacturer, and year of issue.

Sound Recordings

> Ellington, Duke, conductor. *Concert For the Philippines*. Duke Ellington Orchestra. Recorded 13 Feb. 1945. Columbia, 1979.
>
> Seger, Bob. *Bob Seger's Greatest Rock Ballads*. Capitol, 2014.
>
> Wilkerson, Lynn. *The Evolution of Music*. Performed by Andrew Folin and Kyle Clemmons. EMI, 1978.

- For a specific song, list the song title in quotation marks.

> King, B. B. "Rollin' Stones." Recorded 12 May 1956. *King of Blues*. Chess, 2015.

## Film or Videos

- In general, list the title (italicized), director (producer, choreographer), performers, distributor, and year of release.

Film or Videos

> *Living For Tomorrow*. Directed by Mitchell Shockey. Performed by David Reed, Christopher Cadjun, Tia Presnal, and Paul Gellstone. Miramax, 2013.

## Performance (concert, opera, ballet, or play)

- In general, list the title (italicized), significant individuals (playwright, writer, director, performers, etc.), performance site (theater and city), and performance date.

Performances

> *Hamlet*. By William Shakespeare. Directed by Dennis Hartsig. Performed by Michael Donnell and Angela Wilmer. Magic Bag Theater, 5 Apr. 2014.

## Interviews (broadcast, published, or recorded)

**Interviews**

- In general, list the person interviewed, interview title (in quotation marks -- otherwise list *Interview* or *Interview with...*), interviewer may be added if known, interview source (italicized -- program, publication, or recording), interview date (day, month, and year), and pages (if applicable).

> Fonda, Angela. "Running a Successful Business Interview." *Meet The Entrepreneur.* ABC. WABC, 12 Aug. 2014.
>
> Boscarino, Jane. Interview. *New York Times,* 11 Dec. 2013, early ed.: B12.
>
> Brinser, Harold. Interview with Cindy Harsbaugh. *Radio Nation.* National Public Radio. WEDQ, 27 May 2014.

## Personal Interviews (Personal Communication)

**Personal Interviews**

- In general, if the researcher conducted the interview, list the name of the person interviewed and the type of interview (*personal interview, e-mail interview, telephone interview*) and the date(s).

> Eckert, J. M. Telephone interview. 23 Dec. 2015.
>
> Kilpatrick, K. K. Personal interview. 22 July 2015.
>
> Peters, Michael F. E-mail interview. 9-11 May 2015.

## Lectures or Speeches

**Lectures or Speeches**

- In general, list the presenter (lecturer or speaker), presentation title (in quotation marks), meeting, sponsoring organization, presentation location, presentation date (day, month, and year), and descriptive label (*address, lecture, reading,* etc.).

> Mihalec, Alan. "Computer Systems for Newspaper Delivery." Distribution Forum. National Newspaper Convention, 17 Nov. 2014, Palmer House Hotel, Chicago. Address.

## Legal Sources (acts)

- In general, list act name, Public Law number, date of enactment (day, month, and year), and Statutes at Large cataloging number.

> Transportation Equity Act. Pub. Law 105-178. 9 June 1998. Stat. 113.345.

## CD (non-periodical publication)

- In general, list the author (if no author, then list editor, complier, or translator if available), article (essay or poem) that is part of work (in quotation marks), publication title (italicized), editor (if relevant), edition (if relevant), publisher, and publication year.

> Chudzik, Stanley S. "The Real Country Near Dunsinane." *Macbeth*. By William Shakespeare. Edited by Gail Hanko. Sampsell, 2013.
>
> *Encyclopedia of Europe*. McCallister, 2014.
>
> "Macaroni and Cheese Recipes." *Encyclopedia of Processed Foods*. 2nd ed. Parker, 2014.
>
> Michaels, Joseph, editor. *On the Packing Room Floor*. Gale, 2015.
>
> Sippl, Paul. *Navy Supporting Roles*. Hartsig, 2014.

## CD (periodically published database)

- In general, list printed source author (if available), printed source article (if available—in quotation marks), printed source periodical (italicized), volume number (if available), printed source publication date, printed source pages (if available), database (italicized), vendor (if significant), electronic publication date.

> Hennessy, John Thomas. "Native Americans and Teams: Qualitative Research in a Northern Michigan Casino." *Journal of Social Norms,* vol. 21, 2014, pp. 125-29. *Periodical Abstracts* Ondisc. UMI-Proquest. Apr. 2014.
>
> United States Senate. Committee on Fair Trade. *Report on Canadian Trade.* 13 Feb. 2013. 117th Congress. 2nd session. *Senate Masterfile.* Senate Information Service. Dec. 2014.

## Internet Sites (including professional websites)

- List URL that is copied in full from the web browser. Omit *http://*.

- In general, list author (compiler, director, editor, etc.), title (italicized if independent or in quotation marks if part of a larger work), title of overall website if different than title (italicized), version or edition (if applicable), publisher or sponsor, publication date (if available), and page numbers (if available).

> *Advertising Institute of America.* "Making Podcast Commercials." *Podcast Nation,* www.jotadvertisers.com/culture/2016/04/aiat-on-podcasts.
>
> Solarz, Michael E. "Funding Your Retirement" *Wealth Information Page,* 24 May 2014, www.wip.com/support/howto/retire/researchpoint/mgnpimportdata.html.

## Personal Home Pages

- In general, list creating individual, site title italicized (or if no title write *Home page* [not italicized]), date of last update (if available), access date, and URL.

**Personal Home Pages**

> Harcourt, Jeffery. Home page. 28 July 2015, www.it.tsu. edu:6607/jeff/.

## Online Books

- In general, list authors (if no author, list editor, compiler, or translator), title (italicized), editor (compiler or translator), original publisher, original publication year, Internet site (italicized), site editor, version, electronic publication date, sponsoring organization (or institution), and URL.

- If all of this information cannot be found, list whatever is available.

**Online Books**

> Cyman, Patricia R. *Watchful Eyes of Society*. Edited by Annette Birko. 2013. *American Security Information Page,* www.asipnow.org/art/whe/445.445/cf.
>
> Diegel, Karen, and Lisa Shankie. *Socialist Perspectives on War,* 2014. *United Women for Justice.* Edited by Janet LaLonde, 2014. U of Oregon, www.uo.edu/forc/ddt/9980/td.

## Portions of Online Books

- In general, follow the guidelines for online books, but insert the title or name of the portion (in quotation marks) between the author and title.

- If the portion is a standard division of the book (introduction, foreword, afterword, etc.), insert the actual word (*introduction, foreword, afterword*, etc.) between the author and title.

> Houghton, 2013. *Math Grant Research*. Edited by Mark Kaltz, 2014. Florida State U, www.fsu.edu/lit/mmc/9774/.
>
> Usler, Raymond. "Cross Country Training." *German High School Sporting Events*. Translated by Kirk R. Shankie, 2014. *Global High School Sports*. Edited by Paul Hazard, 2014. U of Texas, www.ut.edu/okku/bok/4997/.

## Online Government Publications

- In general, if the author, editor, or compiler is known, list first (unless the agency bears more importance, then the author, editor, or compiler goes after the title).

- If the author, editor, or compiler is unknown, list the issuing government agency first.

- Conclude with the title (italicized), original publisher, original publishing year, and URL.

> United States. Dept. of Agriculture. Office of Food Safety and Inspection Service. *Preventing Listeria in RTE Meat*. GPO, 2013. www.gpo.gov/doc/ovr/6779/.
>
> United States. Dept. of Energy. Office of Natural Resources Preservation. *Alternatives to Oil*. By Howard L. Weinberger, 2015. www.dee.gov/tru/hmj/8890/.
>
> VanderHill, Donald, ed. *List of DNR Approved Consultants for Hunting Safety*. McGraw, 2014, www.dnr.gov/dds/era/8778/.

## Online Journals

- In general, list the author(s), article title (in quotation marks), journal title (italicized), volume number, issue number (or other identifying number), publication year, page numbers (paragraphs or other sections if they are numbered), and URL.

- See the section *When Listing by Author(s)* for one author, multiple authors, multiple citations by the same author(s), multiple citations by the same first author, unknown or anonymous author(s), and unknown or anonymous author(s) with no publisher.

> Dickerhoff, Lori. "Age Factors in Marriage." *Marriage and Family Quarterly*, vol. 11, Nov. 2015, pp. 112-23, www.jmfq.com/raw/rte/9221/.

- If the journal is from a database, state the database (italicized).

> Roddy, Juliette K. "Economics of Northern Michigan Indian Tribes." *Native American Review*, vol. 21, 2014, pp. 291-304. *Academic OneFile*, www.onefile.com/libraries/academic/databases/.

- If a DOI is used, cite the DOI in place of a URL.

> Barnes, Jason T. "Modern Dance in Japan." *Dance Quarterly*, vol. 12, no. 2, Dec. 2015. Crosstown, doi:10.1345/pmc.3000.5642.

## Online Scholarly Project

- In general, list the title (italicized), editor (if available), publication year, sponsoring organization (or institution), and URL.

> *Reconstruction of the Edmund Fitzgerald Tragedy*. Edited by Pelka T. Torte, 2015. U of Minnesota, www.uminn.edu/shi/wri/7679/.

## Online Newspapers

- In general, list the author (if signed), article title (in quotation marks), newspaper (italicized), publication date (complete day, month, and year), and URL.

Shackelford, Molly. "Waste in American Grocery Stores." *New York Times on the Web*, 14 June 2014, www.nytw.com/ayy/tre/88/.

Wilson, Daniel G. "Computer Programs for Tax Preparation." *Detroit News*, 7 Oct. 2015, www.detroitnews.com/art/dai/9981/.

## Online Magazines

- In general, list the author (if signed), article title (in quotation marks), magazine title (italicized), publication date (complete day, month, and year if available), and URL.

Edgeworth, Thomas P. "Turning Sales Ideas into Profit." *Newsmaker.com,* 23 Oct. 2014, www.newsmaker.com/sales/auth/554/.

Sims, Bernice. "Calculators for High School Students in Advanced Math." *Education and Technology Online*, Jan. 2014, www.eto.com/change/auth/9932/.

## Online Reviews (of books, performances, or films)

- In general, list the reviewer (if there is one), title of review (in quotation marks, if there is one), *Review of* title of the work reviewed (italicized), author (editor, translator, director, etc. if available) of the work reviewed, online source (italicized—newspaper, magazine, etc.), review date (day, month, and year if available), and URL.

Neilson, James M., and Donald St. Pierre. Review of *Friends Forever: How Rugby Changed My Life*, by Thomas Diem. *Albuquerque Times Online*, 12 July 2014, www.ato.com/ff/rev/3451/.

Wilhelm, Jeffrey L. "Superheroes of Classic Rock." Review of *American Destiny: The English Musical Invasion.* Edited by David Knapp. *London Book Review*, 23 Aug. 2014, www.lbrr.com/super/rev/4435/.

## Online Anonymous Articles

- In general, list article title (in quotation marks), online source (italicized -- newspaper, magazine, etc.), publication date (complete day, month, and year), and URL.

Online
Articles

> "Global Warming Affects Local Polar Bears." *Alaskan Gazette*, 26 May 2014, www.alagaz.com/gw/opi/3266/.
>
> "Happier Days in Iraq." *Worldnews.com*, 26 Mar. 2015, www. worldnews.com/event/nnrt/6659/.

## Online Editorials

- In general, list the author (if signed), title (in quotation marks), source (italicized—newspaper, magazine, etc.), publication date (complete day, month, and year), and URL.

Online
Editorials

- List *Editorial.* after the title (before source).

> "Dancing for Profit." Editorial. *Chicago Tribune*, 27 Oct. 2015, www.chictrib/pro/art/8845/.
>
> Robichau, Regina. "Investing Takes Discipline." Editorial. *Financialwealth.com,* 17 Aug. 2015, www.finwealth.com/mon/cht/6395/.

## Online Letter to Editor

- In general, list the author (if signed), title (in quotation marks if available), source (italicized -- newspaper, magazine, etc.), publication date (complete day, month, and year), and URL.

Online
Letters

- List *Letter.* after the title (before source).

> Bevac, Louis. Letter. *Alabama Herald Online*, 23 Nov. 2014, www.Alherald.com/edi/ltt/7744/.
>
> Wellsworth, Amanda E. "Reform Our Public Schools." Letter. *New York Times on the Web*, 6 May 2015, www.nytw.com/shco/lem88=t/.

## Online Interviews

- In general, list the person interviewed, interview title (in quotation marks—otherwise list *Interview* or *Interview with...* ), interviewer may be added if known, interview source (italicized—program, publication, or recording), interview date (day, month, and year), and URL.

LeVellier, Kenneth. "Problem Resolution in Family Owned Businesses Interview." *Meet the Entrepreneur Online*, 13 Nov. 2015, www.meetlive.com/bus/res/6=456/.

Normile, Edward. Interview with Edward C. Zoldak. *American Radio on the Web*, 12 Mar. 2014, www.americanweb.com/sal/int/994.4556/.

Trombley, Isadore T. Interview. *Parker Works,* 13 Oct 2015, www.parkerworks.com/llz/tip/55=543.1/.

## Online Television or Radio Programs

- In general, list significant individual(s), segment title (in quotation marks), program title (italicized), network, call letters of station, broadcast date (day, month, and year), and URL.

Warszak, Alfred. "Fresh Water Issues in the Florida Panhandle." *Natural Resource Usage Report.* CBS Radio. WCBS, 13 Mar. 2015, www.wcbs.com/tel/uur/6.787/.

## Online Paintings or Sculptures

- In general, list artist, piece title (italicized), published date, location, and URL.

Danielson, Patricia. *Perfect Human Body Display,* 2014, Presnal Gallery, www.presnalgallery.com/tri/anc/66=435./.

## Online Poems

- In general, list author, title (in quotation marks), published date, and URL.

> Lentz, Stephen L. "The Seeds of Life," 2013, Jan. 2015, www.
> rtu.edu/poetry/seeds/2013.

## Online Maps

- In general, list title (in quotation marks), source (italicized —organization or institution), and URL.

- List *Map* after the title.

> "Myrtle Beach, South Carolina." Map. *U.S. Gazetter.* U.S.
> Census Bureau, 28 Nov. 2014, www.uscensus.gov/map/
> org/8.99=23/.

## Online Cartoons

- In general, list cartoonist, title (in quotation marks), source (italicized—organization or institution), publication date, and URL.

- List *Cartoon* after the title.

> Kelly, William. "The Martins." Cartoon. *Montgomery News
> Online*, 22 July 2014, www.montnews.com/car/trq/56867/.

## Online Advertisements

- In general, list the advertisement and URL.

- List *Advertisement* after the ad name.

> Hiller's Miracle Carpet Cleaning Powder. Advertisement, 23
> Aug. 2015, www.adsrus.com/hil/car/99.931/.

## E-mail Communication

- In general, list writer's name, message title (from subject line [in quotation marks], if available), message description (including recipient), and posting date.

> Jackman, David M. "Re: Locker Partners in School." Received by Thomas J. Horton, 21 Sept. 2014.

## Twitter

- In general, list the tweet in place of the title (in quotation marks), date of tweet, time of tweet, and URL.

> @simbiosa. "Lots of people having fun at the game - #State-football." Twitter, 24 May 2016, 1:15 p.m., twitter.com/simbiosa/status/3394307643.

# Part Four

## Sample Paper

The following excerpts come from an article titled, *Academic Dishonesty*. They were reprinted with permission from the author, Dr. Michael E. Heberling. Some changes have been made to the original document to adhere to the MLA standards described in this handbook. Because only portions of the text have been retrieved, the reading is not verbatim from the actual article. References have been altered and may not be actual accessible resources.

The paper is double-spaced with one-inch margins, though it might not appear that way in this publication due to typesetting.

**½" margin for running head**

**Author's name Professor's name Course name and number Date (day, month, year)**

Michael E. Heberling

Professor McDowell

English 320

8 May 2016

**Paper title**

Academic Dishonesty and the Internet

**Authors and page in parenthetical citation**

Cheating is a serious problem in today's educational system (McCabe et al. 29). The ubiquitous Internet has made it extremely easy for today's students to pirate everything from one-paragraph writing assignments to complete essays. Some students, in fact, might not even view this Internet plagiarism as being wrong. They have been raised on the premise that it is permissible to freely copy songs and movies from the Internet (another fallacy, of course), so they think it is perfectly

**Double-space entire document**

legitimate to copy someone else's words and ideas. They see the Internet as a free and powerful source for the dissemination of knowledge, and they do not see any problem in using this free knowledge for their own work. Students may think it might be wrong to submit a complete paper they had

**1" margins around entire document**

purchased off the Internet, but they do not see anything wrong with utilizing uncited quotations from different authors.

Has the Internet created and encouraged a new cheating tool which students can utilize? While there may never be a definitive answer to this somewhat philosophical question, there can be some educated assumptions based on existing literature. In the article,

**Article title in text**

"Ten Updated Principles of Academic Integrity,"

McCabe and Pavela indicate younger students may not realize the Internet is a relatively new resource tool (10-12). They note it is the faculty member's responsibility to educate students about Internet etiquette as well as its proper use. Internet utilization is a wonderful resource technique, but when abused, the Internet can be discouraging and even detrimental to one's educational experience.

McCabe and Pavela also indicate some faculty have almost abandoned writing assignments because cheating is so rampant ("Ten" 14-16). This is a disservice to the students because reading and writing are, in the author's opinion, two of the most important components of an education. To abandon writing assignments merely limits students in their academic growth and development.

Christina Stolarz wrote an article in the *Detroit News* that explored how many of today's students feel about plagiarism. One sixteen-year-old student said she realized plagiarism was cheating, but that did not stop her from using several copied phrases from the Internet. What was her excuse? She needed the information for her paper but did not want to take the time to properly credit the sources. Her only concern was turning in the paper in a timely manner (1A).

A student who simply purchases or copies a complete paper from the Internet and turns it in as his or her own work deserves no sympathy whatsoever. He or she has cheated in the worst possible way and should be punished by failure of the course and/or expulsion from the program (Simboli 21).

Author in text

Newspaper title in text

Page only in parenthetical citation

However, what about the student who completed substantial original research, but plagiarized by using improperly cited quotations from different sources? He or she obviously put forth considerable effort, but proper citation is still an issue. Should punishment for this particular offense be less severe?

Lastly, what about the student who attempts to give credit in an imprecise way but simply does not do enough work to establish his or her sources? For example, that student might cite a recent editorial in a local newspaper but does not list the author, editor, date, or page number. Is this a form of plagiarism, or is it just lazy writing?

Richard Posner writes:

> ...most plagiarists are obscure, in fact most are students; an estimated one-third of all high-school and college students have committed plagiarism or a closely related form of academic fraud, such as purchasing a term paper from a 'paper mill' (8).

While there is substantial existing evidence related to the prevalence of academic dishonesty, there is, fortunately, a silver lining. Some academic institutions have implemented a traditional or modified honor code. These codes are being incorporated in an effort to reduce the amount of cheating.

In the article, "Some Good News about Academic Integrity," McCabe and Pavela define traditional and modified honor. They state "traditional academic honor codes include written pledges that students sign attesting their work integrity ... Modified honor codes involve judicial roles for students that do not mandate the use of pledges ..." (34).

McCabe and Pavela found institutions that implement traditional or modified honor codes have experienced some success. While cheating is not entirely eliminated, it is significantly reduced when some form of honor code is practiced ("Some Good News," 34-35).

Use shortened version of title in parenthetical citation

The author is acutely aware that cheating, such as plagiarism, is not an absolute thing and cannot be resolved in an absolute way. Educators now have tools, such as Turnitin.com, which enable them to detect plagiarism from the Internet. Consider a scenario in which Turnitin.com results indicate that student A plagiarized 60 percent of his or her paper, and student B plagiarized only 20 percent of his or her paper. Should the punishment be the same for both students?

If the answer is "yes," the assumption is that there is no relativity in plagiarism. Stealing one word or phrase is as bad as stealing an entire paper. Unfortunately, if this rationale were applied to the world outside academia, it would be like saying that stealing a candy bar is just as serious as stealing a million dollars.

If the answer is "no," there must be an attempt to find meaningful and uniform standards by which teachers can evaluate different levels of plagiarism. If every single paper graded by every single teacher could be evaluated by a percentage system such as the one used by Turnitin.com, this might be possible. But this sort of universal grading is not likely to happen in one's lifetime. Also keep in mind, the percentage, while helpful, is not a fail-safe method, and the Turnitin.com report stills requires comparison with the essay and interpretation by the teacher.

However, even resource tools such as Turnitin. com are not foolproof. For example, Turnitin.com only searches online databases and Internet resources. If students utilize both online and print resources, only those used from online sources are considered when attempting to detect any type of plagiarism. Furthermore, if the student utilizes only print resources (not online), such as textbooks, Turnitin.com might be a useless detection device.

While educators should certainly be cognizant of academic dishonesty, such as plagiarism, they also have the responsibility to first educate their students on the very concept of academic dishonesty and plagiarism. First and foremost, what actually constitutes academic dishonesty should be clearly defined for the students.

The suggestion is instructors specifically detail, in their respective syllabi, a section titled something such as "Academic Integrity." In this portion of the syllabus, the instructor should clearly state his or her integrity expectations. Plagiarism should be defined. Further, it is encouraged that instructors note that they have access to online plagiarism detection programs (such as Turnitin.com) and all student work is subject to submission to these various services.

Some instructors have students submit drafts to these services to preview their own reports to inform revisions prior to handing in the final draft.

Finally, the academic dishonesty issue should be discussed during the first week of every class. In *Plagiarism in Higher Education*, the United States Department of Education indicates that students who understand the meaning of academic integrity from the start of the course tend to submit much more original work throughout the entire course.

Title in text

Academic dishonesty will likely always exist in some form. There are certain techniques, however, that deter the likelihood of occurrence.

Works Cited

McCabe, Donald, and Gary Pavela. "Some Good News about Academic Integrity." *Change,* vol. 33, no. 5, 2015, pp. 32-28.

---. "Ten Updated Principles of Academic Integrity." *Change,* vol. 36, no. 3, 2014, pp. 10-16.

McCabe, Donald, et al. "Dishonesty in Academic Environments." *Journal of Higher Education,* vol. 72, 2015, pp. 29-35.

Posner, Richard A. *The Little Book of Plagiarism.* Random House, 2017.

Simboli, Martin Trevor. "Plagiarism: Severe Consequences in Academia." *Journal of Education,* vol. 25, no. 3, 2014, pp. 17-28. www.eric.ed.gov/contentdelivery/servlet/ERICServlet?accno=EJ909069.

Stolarz, Christina. "Schools' New Target: Cybercheaters – Michigan Districts Crack Down on Web Savvy Students Who Think Online Plagiarism is OK." *Detroit News,* 2 Oct. 2016, early ed., p. A1.

United States, Department of Education, Office of Postsecondary Education. *Plagiarism in Higher Education,* 2015. www.doe.gov/postsecondary/plagiarism.html.

Same authors, multiple citations

Journal retrieved online

Newspaper

Government document retrieved online

# Index

# O

# P

# Q

# R

# S

# T

# U

# V